# "THE WORLD'S EASIEST POCKET GUIDE"

### — TO —

# Buying
## Your First
# Car

D0872555

# "THE WORLD'S EASIEST POCKET GUIDE"

## TO

# *Buying Your First Car*

# LARRY BURKETT

## WITH ED STRAUSS
## ILLUSTRATED BY KEN SAVE

NORTHFIELD PUBLISHING
CHICAGO

**Larry Burkett's Money Matters For Kids**
Executive Producer: *Allen Burkett*

**For Lightwave Publishing**
Managing Editor: *Elaine Osborne*
Project Assistant: *Ed Strauss*
Text Director: *Christie Bowler*
Art Director: *Terry van Roon*
Desktop Publisher: *Andrew Jaster*

**ISBN: 1-881273-95-4**

1 3 5 7 9 10 8 6 4 2

*Printed in the United States of America*

# Table of Contents

# How to Use This Book

Shortly after leaving home, many teens and young adults embark on a learning curve so drastic that it resembles a roller-coaster ride. Things they never did before—such as operating a washing machine, paying bills, shopping for groceries, renting an apartment, using a credit card—suddenly become sink-or-swim survival skills. Most teens fail to learn these basics while still at home and are woefully unprepared for life in the real world when they move out on their own.

The four books in this series—*Getting Your First Credit Card*, *Buying Your First Car*, *Renting Your First Apartment*, and *Preparing For College*—were written to fill these gaps in modern education and to teach you the basic life skills you need to survive in today's jungle. In this series we walk you step-by-step through buying a used car without being conned, using a credit card without diving into debt, going to college without mortgaging your future away, and renting an apartment without headaches.

These books contain a wealth of commonsense tips. They also give sound advice from a godly, biblical perspective. It is our prayer that reading the books in this series will save you from having to learn these things in the school of hard knocks.

To get the most out of these books, you should photocopy and complete the checklists we've included. They're provided to help you take on these new tasks step-by-step and to make these books as practical as possible.

Each book contains a glossary to explain commonly used terms. If at any point while reading you need a clear definition of a certain word or term, you can look it up. Each book also contains a helpful index that allows you to find every page where a key word or subject is mentioned in the book.

## CHAPTER 1

# Do You Need a Car?

# Do You Need a Car?

## Teens On Wheels

Ever since the invention of the wheel, teens have had an affinity with speed and power. Some say it all began in the Neanderthal camp the day sixteen-year-old Og came flying down the hill on top of a huge stone wheel, pulled out onto the freeway (everything was free back then), and passed a herd of woolly mammoths in the fast lane.

Thousands of years later, Assyrian teens had perfected the art of doing wheelies with their dads' war chariots. In the Bible, Jehu was such a fast, reckless chariot driver that the lookouts watching him said, "The driving is like that of Jehu son of Nimshi—he drives like a madman" (2 Kings 9:20). Some things never change.

## Today's Big Question

Food, clothing, and shelter are the basic material needs for human beings, but in North America we've added another need to the list: the need for a car. It often is a genuine need. People have to get to work and back somehow. But for a majority of Americans, cars are not just a means of transportation; they have also become an expensive fashion statement.

Fashion is fine, but today's big question is "Do you *need* a car?" A car is expensive, and most young adults can't pay cash for one if it costs more than a few hundred dollars.

## Cars Are Expensive!

If you're a natural grease monkey and your idea of fun is spending every weekend on your back beneath a car, maybe you *can* afford to pick up a junker for a few hundred dollars and keep it repaired and on the road. But *most* new drivers can't do it themselves and have to take their car to a garage to have repairs done. And an old junker that needs con-

8

stant repairs can get expensive pretty quickly.

Rather than buying a car that constantly breaks down, you're better off to buy a new car that needs *no* repairs or a good secondhand car that needs *few* repairs. Both are expensive. According to J. D. Power & Associates (an international market research firm), a new car costs, on the average, about $19,000 and a *good* secondhand car costs approximately $10,000. For teens and young adults, this is *the* biggest expense they'll have.

## Consider Alternatives First

There are several alternatives to buying a car. Which one you choose depends on where you live, how far away your workplace is, and the availability of public transportation. For example, if you live in a large urban area with an excellent subway and bus system, a car is not only expensive but probably unnecessary. And wherever else you need to go, you can get there by foot or on bicycle. The exercise will do you good.

If you can arrange for a friend to pick you up and take you to work every day or to church on Sunday and you just chip in for gas, car pooling is a good alternative. What about going to out-of-the-way places? You can always ask to borrow your parents' car. But if your workplace is some distance away and you need to go to out-of-the-way places regularly, then a car is actually a necessity.

If you do need a car, let's go forward. If you don't, you can still choose a time when you will, and start planning now; and that plan should include setting aside money each month in an account specially designated "Future Car Purchase." Even if you can't save up enough to buy the car outright, you *must* at least save enough to make the initial down payment.

# Monthly Income & Expenses

**Annual Income** _____
**Monthly Income** _____

**LESS**
**1. Charitable Giving** _____
**2. Tax** _____

**NET SPENDABLE INCOME** _____

**3. Housing (30%)** _____
    Mortgage (Rent) _____
    Insurance _____
    Taxes _____
    Electricity _____
    Gas _____
    Water _____
    Sanitation _____
    Telephone _____
    Maintenance _____
    Other _____

**4. Food (17%)** _____

**5. Auto(s) (15%)** _____
    Payments _____
    Gas & Oil _____
    Insurance _____
    License _____
    Taxes _____
    Maint/Repair/
      Replacement _____

**6. Insurance (5%)** _____
    Life _____
    Medical _____
    Other _____

**7. Debts (5%)** _____
    Credit Cards _____
    Loans & Notes _____
    Other _____

**8. Enter. / Recreation (7%)** _____
    Eating Out _____
    Trips _____
    Baby-sitters _____
    Activities _____
    Vacation _____
    Other _____

**9. Clothing (5%)** _____

**10. Savings (5%)** _____

**11. Medical Expenses (5%)** _____
    Doctor _____
    Dental _____
    Drugs _____
    Other _____

**12. Miscellaneous (6%)** _____
    Toiletry, Cosmetics _____
    Beauty, Barber _____
    Laundry, Cleaning _____
    Allowances, Lunches _____
    Subscriptions, Gifts _____
      (Incl. Christmas)
    Special Education _____
    Cash _____
    Other _____

**TOTAL EXPENSES** _____

Net Spendable Income _____

Difference _____

# CHAPTER 2

# How Much Can You Afford?

"I could make this work, no problem! Imagine me... in a new car."

"Read the fine print, girl! With this payment, you'll have this thing paid off when you're fifty!"

# How Much
# Can You Afford?

## Before You Buy

OK, you've decided you do need a car. But the first question you should ask yourself is not "What's my favorite make and model?" or "What color Corvette would I look best in?" but "What can I *afford*?" Yeah, I know, realism in such big doses is apt to deal a deathblow to a great daydream, but cars are very expensive toys and the sooner we achieve "wake-up" and examine the hard, cold facts of life, the better off we'll be.

But even the question, "What can I afford?" has become a bit vague. These days, eighteen-year-old students carry credit cards and are eligible for financing for a car. The possibilities seem wide open; the commercials tell you just how *low* the monthly payments are, and you get a pretty heady feeling of power and begin to think that you can afford . . . well . . . just about *anything!* Sorry, but it just ain't so.

## Low Monthly Payments?

The promise of low monthly payments is a very popular gimmick in car sales these days. But it *is* a gimmick. And what salespeople don't tell you up front is that such a "deal" will require either a hefty down payment (money you probably don't have), or an extended period of repayment, which will cost you thousands of dollars of interest in the long run.

Nevertheless, this kind of advertising is particularly popular with young buyers because of the instant gratification of owning a new car. Who cares if the payments last seven years and the car only lasts five? Well, *you* will during the last two years! Also be aware that the period of low payments may only last for a short time—two or three months—

and then they'll increase in size to make up for the lower payments you started with.

## No Money Down

"No money down! No car payments till 2003!" I'm sure you've heard that pitch. But before you sign on the dotted line, read the fine print. Have you ever noticed how *big* the letters are when a salesperson is screaming the sales pitch?—but how *small* the exact details are when you see one of those cars advertised on TV?

Next time, tape one of those ads with your VCR, then play it back, freeze the frame, and read the lightning-quick fine print to see how much you're really going to save. Your "zero down, no payments for a year" deal will probably carry a very high percentage rate, being computed all during the months that you're not making payments. Then you'll actually owe *more* than the original price once your payments start. Once again, the warning is true: If it sounds too good to be true, it probably is.

## What's Your Income?

Instead of asking "What can I afford?" ask yourself "What's my monthly income? What's left over after all my regular expenses?" Looking at things that way may not exactly cause limitless vistas of possibilities to open up, but it'll keep you out of debt and save you from having your shiny new car snatched by the credit company when you can no longer make the monthly payments.

If you're living on your own and paying for housing, food, and utilities, we recommend that you spend no more than 15 percent of your disposable income (net income after taxes and giving to God) on an automobile. This not only includes the monthly payments, but gas, insurance, and repairs too. (Check with your state, county, and municipality for other applicable taxes.) These are tried and proven guidelines, and while they may vary slightly in individual cases, it is not in your interest to disregard them. If you want a shiny new sports car, you may think you can cut your food bill in half, allowing you to spend 25 percent of your income on car payments, but that's not wise.

An easy way to figure out what you can afford is to photocopy the budget form on page 10 and fill in the blanks. Once you've filled in all the other spaces for your regular monthly expenses, what do you have left? What amount can you put in your transportation spot and not feel like a slave to the payments?

Unless you buy a car with zero money down, you'll have to put down a fairly substantial down payment. This should come from your savings. "*What* savings," you ask? Well, before you left home, you should have set aside as much money as you could each month in anticipation of this day. If you haven't, start now.

# What Kind of Car?

You may wonder, "What kind of a car does God want me to have? Can I drive a Ferrari?" We're not talking about what make of a car. We're talking about value. For somebody who has the funds, who doesn't have to borrow the money, it may be that a new, more expensive car is a better buy. If you bought a Mercedes, then drove that car for ten or twelve years, that car would cost you less than if you had purchased three or four less expensive cars during the same time.

OK, so you're not getting the Mercedes. But you get the point. It's mostly a decision between you and the Lord. God doesn't say, "Buy a Chevrolet," or "Buy a Ford." God generally says, "Using God-given wisdom, it's a good idea to buy what's within your ability to pay for. And, ideally, you should be able to pay cash for it." Remember, "Buy the best value for you." (See chapter 5, "Upkeep And Money Drain.")

# CHAPTER 3

# Look at Your Options

"Uh... well... hee, hee...
a minor detail..."

# Look at Your Options

Now that you know how much money you have to work with, what can you get with it? Used car or new? Which is actually the better buy?

## Buying a New Car

***Sudden depreciation.*** Obviously, there are benefits to owning a new car. No previous owners have worn it out; it has no accident history; it has a full warranty, etc. You can get a slightly better financing rate because new cars are worth more than used cars, so banks will always give you a lower interest rate on a loan for a new car than they will on a loan for a used car. And new cars smell pretty good inside. But you need to ask yourself how *much* you're willing to pay for that new car smell and the fact that no one has driven the car before you bought it.

The problem is, most new cars lose about 25 percent of their value as soon as you sign the papers. On a $20,000 car, you immediately lose $5,000. As soon as you sign your name, from that point on, you'll always have a debt greater than what the car is worth. And get this! By the end of its first year, your new car will have lost a total of 30 to 40 percent of its original value. If you had to give the car back for any reason or sell it to a third party, you'd still owe the bank more money than the car was worth.

***Getting what you can afford.*** This is not the only thing to consider when you're buying new versus used. You must also be certain that the car you buy will fit in your budget. Jesus said in Luke 14:28, "Suppose one of you wants to build a tower. Will he not first sit down and estimate the cost to see if he has enough money to complete it?" God expects us to not only buy a car that fits our needs, but that is reasonably within our means to pay for.

Young adults with a net income of $12,000 per year

($1,000/month) can afford about $150 a month for *all* car expenses. This includes car payments, tax, maintenance, gasoline, batteries, tires, insurance, everything. They almost *certainly* have to buy a good used car or they'll be buying a car they can't afford. For teens and young adults, buying a good used car is *the* best option.

# Leasing a Car

"Wait a second!" you say. "What about *leasing* a new car? Isn't that an option? Almost every car dealer I talked to asked me if I wanted to lease." They may have asked you, but not because it was in your best interest. The reason dealers urge people to lease is because they make so much *money* through leasing. Leasing is expensive, and in the end you don't even own the vehicle.

Leasing does work for some people. If you have lots of money and always want to drive the newest model car, then getting one car after another on a two- or three-year lease is a good way to accomplish that. Or if you *only* want to drive vehicles covered by the manufacturer's warranty, a three-year lease on a vehicle with a three-year warranty will do the trick—but at a price most of us cannot afford.

There are also penalties that most people are unaware of, such as early payoff penalties and extra mileage penalties. If you decide to pay off your lease early, the penalties will be so high you could have almost *bought* a car instead. And if you drive more than a certain amount—usually 10,000 miles a year—you'll pay an extra amount at the end of the lease. If you're still interested in leasing, the book *Auto Leasing Secrets* by Mark Esselson will tell you everything you need to know before you sign on the dotted line. Or decide not to. We generally advise against teens and young adults leasing a vehicle.

# Buying a Used Car

*Getting a* good *used car.* Many people hesitate to buy a used car because they don't know how to evaluate one. Or they're afraid of being taken advantage of and getting stuck with a junker that needs constant repairs. We'll give some tips in the following chapters on how to look over a used car, but remember, buying a "used" car does not have to mean buying a junker from someone you've never met. Nor do you have to buy a car that's so old that you start it by running with your feet through a hole in the floor, like Fred Flintstone.

If you buy a "new" used car, one with 10,000 to 15,000 miles on it, you won't find many lemons. Many people simply lease a car for a couple years, then trade it in for a new car, so there's not much wear and tear on it.

*More for your money.* Whether you buy one at a car dealership or from a private individual, you'll get a much better car than you could afford to buy new. You'll get more features, electric door locks and air-conditioning and everything else that comes with it *and not have to pay for it.* A simple fact of life is: A used car sells for a lot less than a new car does. Why? Because you're not paying the 25 to 40 percent first-year depreciation that is included in a new car price.

A used car, a one-year-old car, maybe even a two-year-old car, is a better value. Dollar for dollar, you get more value for your money. And the way most automobiles are made today, you're going to get high mileage out of them: 150,000 to 200,000 miles. So 15,000 miles up front isn't going to make a lot of difference.

Of course, even if you're buying a *used* used car—say it's five years old and has 60,000 miles on it—you can still get a good deal if the previous owner took good care of it and gave it regular tune-ups.

# Internet Drives Down Prices

Did you ever wonder why the price of computers and other electronic goods has dropped in recent years but the price of cars keeps going up? This is because in recent years the automobile industry has significantly increased the level of safety, technology, and quality in their vehicles, including stricter emission controls. This has been in response to consumer demands, legislation, and lawsuits. The manufacturers then pass on these costs to the public.

Will the price of cars ever go down? That may take a while. But in the meantime, you can still save thousands of dollars off the sticker price of new cars, and you don't have to enter showrooms or deal with high-pressure salespeople. Countless Americans are saving thousands of dollars on cars right now by shopping on the Internet. According to the CommerceNet and Nielsen Media Research survey conducted in April 1999, some 18.2 million Internet shoppers in North America were buying cars and car parts on-line.

In his book, *Buying and Leasing Cars on the Internet*, Ron Raisglid explains how, when buying a new car, you can avoid paying car dealerships the manufacturer's suggested retail price (MSRP) and can buy a car for only $100 over the manufacturer's invoice price (MIP). That's right! You can buy a new car for only $100 more then the dealer paid for it himself. This represents a saving of several thousand dollars.

# The Wave of the Future

Car dealerships make a much smaller profit on such sales, and, predictably, many see the Internet as a threat and are fighting it. But Internet sales are the wave of the future and dealers need to change or it will sweep them away like a tsunami. In a few years there will be far less high-pressure salespeople in fancy showrooms earning huge commissions. Some dealers have already cut back on high-salaried staff, are selling cars for next to cost, and still making a profit (your $100 plus kickbacks from the manufacturers).

Of course, even if you save $3,000 by buying a new car at invoice price, if that rock-bottom price is $18,000, that's *still* a humongous purchase for a first-time buyer with little or no credit history and few savings. It makes buying a new car

# CHAPTER 4

# Financing Your Purchase

"What's with all this?"

"The bank said they'd loan me the money for that cool superbucket convertible. All I need to do is come up with enough collateral and that baby is mine!"

# Financing Your Purchase

The best way to buy a new or used car is to save the money ahead of time and buy it outright. This way you avoid having to pay literally thousands of dollars in interest charges. On top of it, the money you're saving is actually *earning* interest in a bank in the meantime.

## Interest Rates

If you're like most people, however, you'll have to arrange financing to buy a car, so watch how much interest you'll be paying, because it really adds up. Find the best interest rates by shopping around. Find out what *your* bank is offering, then find out what *other* banks and savings and loans are offering. A credit union will generally give you a better rate than a bank, but you have to be a member first.

Try to avoid dealer-arranged financing. It may seem convenient, but it's the most expensive way to finance a car loan. You can almost always get a better deal if you get a loan elsewhere and just pay the dealer cash for the car.

For long-term loans on purchases such as cars, negotiate a simple interest loan (where you pay a set amount of interest) instead of a compound interest loan (where you pay interest on the interest).

## Down Payments

You usually can't buy a car with 0 percent down, but when you do, it increases the amount of your monthly payment. This, as a result, increases your interest payments. Generally, however, you have to pay a substantial down payment up front, about 10 percent of the total cost of the vehicle. Let's say you're buying a used car for $10,000. You'll need $1,000 in savings to make the down payment. Don't expect the bank to slip in that $1,000 as part of the loan. It wants *you* to pay it so that you have a *personal* stake in your vehicle and won't default on your car payments.

Remember, the more cash you pay up front, the more money you'll save on interest payments. So if you can, it's worth paying more than just the bare minimum.

# Case in Point

Let's say you buy a brand new Sunflower for $19,000. You pay the 10 percent down payment ($1,900) and borrow $17,100 from the bank at 10 percent interest. (You can get lower interest rates on a new car, but 10 percent is a realistic figure.) On a five-year loan, your monthly payments would be $363. In the end, after paying back the loan, you would also have paid $4,715 in interest.

If you had saved up at least *half* the money ($9,500) for the Sunflower, you'd only have to borrow $9,500. On a five-year loan at 10 percent interest, your monthly payments would be $202 and you'd only pay $2,620 in interest.

Let's look at used cars: Say you buy a '97 Windwagon for $10,000. You pay 10 percent ($1,000) down and finance the rest ($9,000) at 12 percent interest. (You won't get as good an interest rate on a used car loan.) If you pay the loan off in three years, your monthly payments would be $299, and the total interest you'd pay would be $1,768.

If you could put down $5,000 in cash and only borrow the other $5,000 at 12 percent interest to buy your Windwagon, your monthly payments would be a mere $166, and at the end of three years, you'd only have paid $982 in interest.

# Collateral

Because cars lose value so rapidly, lenders consider them a high-risk loan. Therefore, they carry a high interest rate. That's why if you have no collateral and have to pledge the car itself as collateral (meaning that the bank reclaims it if you don't pay), you pay very high interest rates. But if you can put something else up as collateral—say you have money in a savings account—you'll get a lower interest rate.

# Trade-ins

If you have a car already, you can sell it and put the money toward your new car. If your old car is in good shape, a car dealer may pressure you to trade it in as part of the deal. This kind of one-stop deal is convenient, but you pay a very high price to enjoy that convenience.

You can usually sell your old car for at least 20 percent more than you would get if you traded it in to a dealership. Why? Because 20 percent is the amount dealers try to undercut by. If the *low* price in the *Kelley Blue Book* for your particular make and model is $6,000, the dealership will traditionally give you no more than $4,000 on a trade-in. (If they can sucker you into accepting even less on a trade-in, it's called "stealing the trade.")

Unless you're an extremely hard-nosed negotiator you're better off selling your car privately and saving $2,000. To find out how much *your* car is worth, look it up in the *Kelley Blue Book* or type your car's vital data on their handy website—***www.kbb.com***—for a tailor-made estimate.

# Cosigning

You'll be tempted to get your dad or some rich relative to cosign for your loan. Don't do it. Cosigning is "surety" and in direct violation of biblical teachings. (See Proverbs 6:1–5; 11:15; 22:26–27.) Cosigning is not a mere formality. If someone cosigns for you, he has made a legal agreement that if you can't keep up the payments for any reason, he will be held liable to pay instead.

# CHAPTER 5

# Upkeep and Money Drain

"Hey... Is she alright? What happened?"

"She just got the estimate on her transmission repair. I think she's gone into shock!"

# Upkeep and Money Drain

You've decided on a car you think you'd like and can afford. But before you dump your life savings into a wheelbarrow and dash down to a dealership, let's add up all the expenses and see what you can actually afford. You may be able to afford the down payment and the monthly payments on a car, but these are only the beginning of what that car will cost you each month.

## Extended Warranties

It's best not to buy an extended warranty. Not only is it expensive, but it's usually not much help. If the dealership wants to sell you a three-year extended warranty, you can be sure they've already fixed whatever problems might go wrong before those three years are up. The problems you hoped the warranty would cover usually won't begin to show up till some time *after* the warranty expires.

The best way to prepare for big repairs is to take the money you would have spent on an extended warranty and, month by month, set it aside in a special "big repairs" account. If you need it, it's there, but chances are good you'll pass the end of the warranty period without touching it. Then, when the big repairs start to arrive and you need money the most, your "big repairs" fund will be there for you.

## Upkeep and Maintenance

Besides car payments, you have to keep gas in your tank, right? How much will that cost? Depending on the gas mileage of your car and how much you drive it, probably between $50 and $100 a month. And don't forget oil, brake fluid, antifreeze for your radiator, windshield washer fluid, and so on. Let's say the total cost is $100/month.

You should also set aside money each month for regular

checkups. This is particularly true if you bought an older used car. If you *don't* set aside money for checkups, you will tend to put off going in for checkups on a regular basis. The result? Small repairs become worse and worse until they explode upon the scene as a major breakdown. To avoid this, take your car to a garage for regular checkups or tune-ups. We'll talk more about this in chapter 10.

# Car Insurance

Car insurance is a "must have." It is not good advice. It is not an option. It is a legal requirement. It may seem like another expense you don't need, but if you bash into someone's shiny new car and have no insurance, you could end up paying him or her $5,000 out of your own pocket. Think how long it would take to pay *that* off!

Laws regulating auto insurance differ from state to state, so find out what the rates are in your state. Insurance costs also vary depending on the car, your age, gender, and years of driving experience. New drivers pay the highest rates, but don't worry. Year after year of accident-free driving will steadily bring your rates down.

Insurance is usually paid once a year, and that's the best way to do it. Before you buy a car, find out what car insurance costs in your state for a driver your age of a used car, then begin saving the money. That way you won't have to finance your insurance and pay interest. And when you pay cash for your car insurance the first time, commit yourself during that whole year to set aside money to cover your next payment. Then when it comes time to pay, you'll again pay in one lump sum and again avoid finance and interest charges.

# American Automobile Association

Should you or should you not belong to the American Automobile Association (AAA)? AAA membership fees vary from state to state but start at about $50 or $60 annually (with a $20 one-time admission fee), and membership has some tremendous benefits, such as four free tow truck services per year. You said you were buying a *used* car? What happens when it breaks down on the highway? You phone a tow truck to take you to the nearest garage and pay anywhere from $50 to $100 depending on the distance. Sounds like you just paid your AAA fees twice over for *one* tow! And what happens *next* time it breaks down? You get the picture. Check them out at ***www.aaa.com***

# Vehicle Emission Checks

Vehicle emission checks or smog checks vary from state to state, and are most stringent in California. If you bought a used car, be aware that in some states, every year when you go to buy insurance, you'll need to take your vehicle to a smog check inspection station. The fee is not large, but if your vehicle fails, you will be required to pay from $50 to $300—depending on its age—to get it into shape so it passes inspection.

# Add It Up

When you're deciding on a car, remember that new cars will give you better gas mileage and burn less oil and need zero to few repairs, whereas an old car will have poorer gas mileage, may need new tires, will burn more oil, and will require more ongoing repairs. Add up the monthly and yearly costs of the car of your choice (including a guesstimate on probable repairs) to get an idea of what your ongoing expenses will be.

# Make Your Plan

After putting aside what you'll need for all the other things in your life and for upkeep, insurance, repairs, and so on for your car, look at what you have left. This is how much you can afford in actual monthly payments. Now ask yourself how much you need to save to buy it outright or make a down payment. How long will it take? For example, if you need to pay $1,000 in a down payment, it would take you ten months at $100 a month to save that amount.

Begin putting aside now what you've slotted into your budget for monthly transportation. If that still won't get you the car you need soon enough, there are ways of raising extra money, apart from taking out a loan. You could take on an extra job, sell your collection of Elvis dolls or some of your other possessions, etc.

# Planning Your Attack

I need $_____ to buy the car outright.

I need $_____ to make a down payment.

I have $_____ saved up.

I am saving $_____ a month extra.

I need a car by _____/_____/_____ (within _____ months).

By then, I'll have $_____ and will need $_____ more.

I'll earn the extra by _____.
(e.g., garage sale, selling stereo or bug collection, etc.)

I'll take on an extra job at $_____ /month.

# CHAPTER 6

# Beware of Sales Gimmicks

# Beware of Sales Gimmicks

## Insider Secrets

A lot of people dread going to a car dealership because they're afraid of being taken advantage of by dishonest salesmen. They fear that slick salespeople will size them up as naive, con them for as much money as they can get, and pile on as many "extra charges" as they can, all to increase their sales commission. We wish we could tell you that these fears are unfounded, but there's actually a lot of truth to them.

Before we give you the lowdown on the deceptive and unethical tricks that some car salespersons use, bear in mind that there are ethical people and Christian men and women selling cars, and there are honest dealerships. These folks do need to make a profit. Most sales staff are working on commission and *must* sell if they want to earn a wage and feed their families.

## Salespeople's Complaints

Customers have legitimate complaints against car salespeople, but salespeople have beefs as well. Experience has shown them that some buyers are liars. Some buyers do not tell the truth about their credit history or trade-ins. Buyers say they'll come back, but never do. Buyers treat them with disrespect. Buyers waste their time looking at cars they can't afford and will never buy. Buyers are late for appointments or break appointments without even bothering to phone to tell them—so salespeople waste their time waiting for someone who doesn't show up when they could have been with other customers.

We're sharing the following information to keep you from getting taken in by unscrupulous salespersons. But remember, as a Christian, you should be polite to *every* person—including salespeople (Matthew 5:13–16).

# Tricks of the Trade

*Laydowns:* Do salesmen size you up when you walk into their showroom? Absolutely! In fact, they have names for different customers. A *laydown* is a customer who accepts all prices at face value with little or no fight, who just "lays down" and lets the dealer walk all over him.

*Pounders:* If they see they've got a real *laydown,* they *really* begin slapping on extra fees. Then you become a *pounder.* A *pounder* is a customer who willingly pays an extra $1,000 *(a pound)* without question. Salespeople love to get two-, three- and even four-pounders. They play on your lack of credit history or savings and count on your inexperience and naïveté.

*The Bump:* After you've agreed on a price, the salesperson, then the sales manager, then the general manager, and finally the finance manager will each inform you of an "additional expense." This is a very common trick and is called *the bump.*

*Wearing You Down:* Car dealers know that negotiating the price on a car is an unpleasant experience and people want to get it over with. So they hand you off from one salesperson to the next and keep you in their showroom. They hope if they keep you for *hours* and wear you down, you won't go to another dealer to repeat this grueling experience, and when they finally send in their top salesperson, you'll cave in and sign the papers. And it works.

*Being Flipped:* By the way, being handed off from one salesperson to the next is called *being flipped.* Sort of like a hamburger. Bet you don't relish that thought.

*Bait and Switch:* It gets worse. Let's say you carefully go over your budget and figure out what kind of car you can afford. Then a really great car is advertised for a low price. You rush down to the car lot but that car is "unavailable." Instead, a salesperson tries to switch your interest to a more expensive car. This practice is not only dishonest; it is illegal.

*Lowballs:* You haggle and haggle but they won't give you a decent price. As you leave, the salesperson throws you a *lowball* and lies, "Come back tomorrow and we'll give it to you for (and here he gives a really low price)." You return the next day only to hear the finance manager tell you that he's under no obligation to honor the salesperson's oral promise.

# Buyer Beware

*Don't Trust Them:* No matter *how* friendly or charming the salesperson is, no matter how good a feeling you get about him or her, be wary. He or she is probably *not* on your side. Salespeople may help steer you toward the kind of car you want, but in many cases, they're *not* trying to help you find a "good deal." Their primary goal is to make a commission on a sale.

*Check Out Everything:* Used car salespeople usually know the problems a car has, but may not tell you. Some unscrupulous dealers outright lie. So check out everything. (See the pointers we give in chapter 8.)

*Distrust the Friendly:* Be suspicious of very friendly salespeople. Profit-minded dealers count on the fact that honest customers want to trust them, want to believe that others are honest and fair. The more you accept them as friends, the more you'll trust them and be willing to pay the high prices they quote.

*Relatives Beware:* Many people go to a dealership because a relative works there and has promised them a "good price." They thought they had an "in," but they still get soaked. In fact, if you intend to do some hard-nosed bargaining, deal with a complete stranger. That way you won't feel guilty about knocking down a relative's profits.

*Drive/Drag Ads:* Don't believe ads that promise that even if you have to *drag* your old junker onto their car lot, they'll give you $2,000 off on a trade-in. They did not go temporarily insane and decide to lose money on a car they can never resell! The $2,000 was *added* to the price before they made this offer.

*Discount Coupons:* Discount coupons are not worth the paper they're printed on. Again, the price was already jacked up before the "discount" was made.

*Slash-It Sales:* A huge ad says that Papa's Auto Lot is having a megasale and slashing all prices! Some cars will go for only $400 dollars!! So you rush down and join the crowds. Balloons are everywhere. But by the end of the morning the balloon bursts and you realize that only a few old clunkers actually sold for $400. All other cars whose prices were "slashed" sold for . . . well . . . pretty much their regular price.

*Take the Test Drive:* There are some perfectly "harmless" ploys, such as urging you to take the new car for a test drive. While this is a legitimate part of the purchasing process, getting behind the wheel of a new car is known to have a practically hypnotic effect on consumers. And it almost always sets you up for increased sales pressure.

# So What Do I Do?

*Hardheaded Negotiations:* Knowing the above may not make buying a car a more pleasant experience, but it can save you hundreds and even thousands of dollars. You may say, "But I don't know the first thing about mechanics, financing, and bargaining." If that's the case, take along a friend or family member who *does*. Afterwards, treat him to a steak dinner as thanks for all the money he saved you. You still should do the footwork, but just commit yourself to walking away from the high-pressure sales tactics without signing anything.

*Voice of Conscience:* Even when you're doing the checking out, it's a good idea to always take a friend with you, even if this other friend doesn't know a lot about mechanics or prices. Tell her she's to be your Jiminy Cricket—"voice of conscience." When she sees you being overpersuaded by a salesperson, she can interrupt by asking lots of questions. Or if she sees you falling in love with a car you shouldn't own, she can blurt out, "Wow! That sure is expensive!"

Then, when you find something you like, call your mechanically inclined, sales-smart family member. Let him play hardball with the dealers and help you get a fair price. Let him avoid the sales tricks and say "no" to the salesperson's every attempt to "bump" up the price. Let him go over the final confusing forms and ask the pointed questions before you sign.

***Buying Agencies:*** If you have no sales-smart friends or relatives, contact a buying agency or an auto broker. For a reasonable fee, you can get a "hired gun" to make your purchase for you. He'll buy any car you wish and resell it to you. Just make sure you find a reputable, licensed broker. It's generally not wise to deal with an unlicensed car expert who is simply freelancing and expects to get paid under the table.

Another very good option is to simply do your foot-work on the Internet. You're not a computer expert either? Find a friend who is, or go to your local library; it usually has study hall access to the Internet. Then get a copy of Ron Raisglid's book, *Buying & Leasing Cars on the Internet,* and go at it.

# CHAPTER 7

# Find the Car

"I told you... That price was too good to believe!"

# Find the Car

## Do Your Research

When you're ready to buy a car, you may have a certain model in mind. Maybe it just looks classy or the design appeals to you. But it's wise to ask mechanically inclined friends or relatives what a good, dependable model of car is, one with good gas mileage and few repair problems. (It may turn out that the fancy sports car you wanted is infamous for some of the most bizarre engine problems imaginable!)

And if you're going to be totally objective about it, ask them to give you several of their top choices. Ask owners of these cars—and similar cars—how they like them, what their maintenance and repair bills are like, etc.

Borrow the *Consumer Report's Complete Guide to Used Cars* or the *Kelley Blue Book* or a similar car value guide from your public library. In Canada, you can also get the *Lemon-Aid Used Cars* books which gives advice on how to avoid buying—you guessed it—lemons. Look up the models your friends suggested, note what the standard prices are, and take careful note of what the main problems and drawbacks are of each model. Keep your research notes in a folder so you don't lose them, and so you can easily refer to them.

There's also a wealth of information on the Internet. A number of good sites will give you the scoop on a particular make of used cars. Among those we recommend are Edmunds at **www.edmunds.com** or the Ultimate Automotive Buyer's Guide at **www.autosite.com**

## Where to Look

The first place to go when looking for a good buy in a used car is to your closest friends and your church. Let them know you're looking for a car. Find out if there's a family in your church who has a car to sell that meets your needs. Before sincere Christians will sell their car to somebody they know, they will either tell them everything that is wrong with it or fix it.

Other sources of good used cars are dealerships that carry "previously owned" cars. You may find a fairly new car that was simply traded in for an even newer vehicle. Or perhaps it was leased for two to three years then returned. Or perhaps it was owned by someone who couldn't make the payments and it was repossessed.

You can also check with leasing companies and your local banker, particularly if you have a Christian banker. Be aware, however, that leased or repossessed cars usually need some repairs. Therefore, you must have some money in reserve for repairs.

A less desirable way to locate a used car is to go through newspaper want ads. The problem with this is that you don't know the person and he doesn't know you, so he has no reason to give you a good deal. In fact, he may even figure he has no reason to be honest with you. Nevertheless, if you must buy a car from an unknown private owner, we give a few tips in chapter 8 to help you determine the value of the car.

There are most likely used cars listed on your local Internet sites. Check them out. The advantage of an Internet "want ads" site is that the seller is not limited to just a couple of expensive sentences, but can describe his or her car in detail and even include a photo.

Last is going to a car auction, which we don't recommend unless you're something of a car expert. You can get some great deals, but you have no idea of the car's history or problems.

# Checklist

If you search in the following places, you're bound to come up with several options.

____ your closest friends

____ newspaper want ads

____ ads on the Internet

____ used car dealerships

____ leasing companies

____ public service bulletins

____ a car auction

____ fellow church members

____ your local banker

____ fellow workers

**CHAPTER 8**

# Make the Purchase— Used Cars

"Well... yer vacuum defibrillator has a positive induction ratio that's makin' yer manifold venturi collapse in the exhaust bearing flow thru ports..."

# Make the Purchase—
# Used Cars

## Knowing the Problems

When you took out the *Consumer Report's Complete Guide to Used Cars,* you probably got it on a four-week loan. So if you're going to be looking at several different cars within one month, hold onto the book so you can check out each prospective car you come across.

When you see an ad in the paper for a 1995 Lubada, check the book. It may say that 1992–96 Lubadas have (a) extensive oil leak problems, (b) wheel bearings and front brake discs that wear out prematurely, and (c) difficulty starting in cold weather. When you phone the owner, instead of asking *if* the vehicle ever has oil leaks, ask, "*What* problems have you had with oil leaks? What shape are the front brake discs in?"

If you don't want to deal with these problems, pass on the Lubada. No car will be perfect, however, and other cars will have their own set of problems. Even if you do get the Lubada, you at least know what problems to expect. And you can use knowledge of these problems when bargaining a lower price with the owner.

## Preliminary Phone Questions

Phoning ahead of time can save you a trip to see a car that's not worth your time. If you don't know much about cars, however, you may hesitate to ask questions that expose your ignorance. So here are some simple but intelligent questions to ask about whichever car you're interested in:

- Is there rust? Where?
- How many miles are on the odometer?
- What's the gas mileage?

- How many previous owners has it had?
- What repairs have you had to make? How recently were they done? How expensive were they? What still needs to be done?
- How are the tires, brakes, window glass?
- What color is it?
- Has it been in any accidents that you know of?

## On the Scene

No used car will be without some problem or weakness, but if you feel the owner has taken care of his vehicle and isn't trying to unload junk, make an appointment for a visit. If you don't know much about cars, it's worth taking along a friend or family member who is knowledgeable. If that doesn't work out, then here are some things to look for to give you a clearer idea of what you're really getting.

Unless you can memorize the following points, you may want to photocopy them and take them with you when you go to see a car. Check each blank after you've looked at that particular part of the car.

# Used Car Checklist

### EXTERIOR

____ Check the wear on the tires. The tread should be at least half an inch deep. Also examine tires for uneven tread wear since this could mean the wheels need to be aligned or that the car frame is bent.

____ Look for oil spots on the driveway or ground where the car has been parked. Check beneath the car for oil dripping from the engine.

____ If the owner said there was rust, ask to see it. Check for covered-up body rust by looking and feeling inside wheel wells.

____ Look down the side of the vehicle and make sure there are no ripples in the body. If there are, some work has probably been done on it.

____ Look for paint that doesn't match (signs of body repair after an accident).

____ Push down on the front and the back bumpers. The car should spring back up and stop. If it bounces a few times, the shock absorbers are shot.

____ Open and close the doors and make sure they shut properly.

____ Feel the antenna, mirrors, gas filler door and cap, and all trim to make sure they're secure.

____ Are there pits or cracks in the windshield? These could develop into large cracks. Have the owner replace the windshield. It's usually covered under his insurance. (In many states, you can't get a license plate if there is a crack in the windshield.)

## INTERIOR

____ Look for different colors of paint inside the door hinges/jams or under the hood. This tells you that the vehicle has been in an accident and been repainted.

____ Turn the key to the first position and check all gauges and warning lights.

____ Test all the lights: headlights, taillights, backup lights, brake lights, turn signals.

____ Test the radio and all its knobs and features.

____ Test the windshield wipers and washer in all settings.

____ Test the fan, heater, air conditioner, defroster, and all vents and switches.

____ Try all dashboard features: switches, levers, ashtray, lighter, glove compartment door.

____ Run all the windows up and down.

____ Adjust the seats in all positions to make sure they move and lock properly.

____ Try all the doors, check the locks; open and latch the trunk and hood.

____ Compare the mileage on the odometer to the wear on the brake pedal. If the odometer says the car has only been driven 40,000 miles but the brake pedal looks worn, the odometer has been tampered with.

____ Check the spare tire in the trunk.

## ENGINE

____ Beware of an engine that's "too clean"—a sign that it may have a major oil leak that's merely been cleaned away rather than repaired.

____ Lift the radiator cap and look for oil that has leaked into the antifreeze. It will be floating on the top.

____ Check that the brake fluid level is high.

____ Pull up the dipstick and check the transmission fluid.

## PAPERS & QUESTIONS

____ Check the maintenance booklet. Has the car faithfully received periodic checks?

____ Look through the ownership books for how many previous owners the vehicle has had, as well as the car's repair history.

____ Ask about previous upkeep and repair costs.

____ Don't buy a used car that is sold without a smog (emmissions) certificate. You could end up paying hundreds of dollars to bring it into compliance or discover that it can't pass inspection. Also, beware of counterfeit certificates.

____ Get the vehicle identification number (VIN) and phone the Department of Motor Vehicles to make sure that there aren't unpaid parking tickets posted against the car. You may end up paying for these if the previous owner didn't.

____ Check the owner's registration and title to be sure the car is registered and owned by the person selling it to you. If the car isn't paid for, the title will show a "lien holder," which means the bank still must sign the title to make the sale.

**THE TEST DRIVE**

____ If you want to take it for a test drive, but the owner refuses, do not—I repeat, *do not*—buy the car. He probably has something to hide.

____ Brake sharply to test the brakes.

____ Listen for unusual or loud engine noises.

____ Check how it turns, and if it "pulls" to one side when driving.

If the vehicle fails a number of these checks, you might not want to buy it. If you still want to buy it, you should use these defects to bargain down the price. Point out that it's going to cost you a lot of money to make all the needed repairs.

# Comparing

If the car and owner seem reliable, thank the seller for his or her time and explain that you have other cars to look at. Avoid making any deal or negotiating until you've looked at several other cars. Walking away helps you to make a more thoughtful decision, and it tells the seller that you're not desperate. If an aggressive seller senses urgency, he'll turn on the pressure to sell and be much less willing to negotiate the price.

# Bargaining

If you're buying a used vehicle from a car dealership, be aware that they generally try to make *twice* as much profit on a used car as they do on a new car. They don't *need* that much profit, so this is a great opportunity for you to do some bargaining and save a lot of money.

Make them a substantially lower offer than their asking price. It is standard procedure for the dealer to turn down the first three offers a buyer makes on a car. No matter *what* your offer is, he says, "That's not enough." Usually the manager will tell the salesperson, "No matter what they offer, add $500 or $1,000 to it." That's a common practice.

Do your research on the year and model of the car so you know what it's worth—let's say in this case $8,000. If they're asking $10,000, make your first bid $6,000. They won't agree, so walk away. You have a great advantage if you're not in a big hurry, because dealerships are usually more eager to sell a car than customers are to buy, so they'll probably phone you the same day or the next day. If not, go back and haggle some more.

If they offer it to you for $9,000, thank them for their time and walk away again. Tell them if they want your business, your final offer is $8,000. They *will* call you again.

# Bargaining Points

It helps greatly if you can point out actual defects to them—which they probably knew about already, but just didn't tell you about. This is where it pays to take the car in to a garage and get it certified. If the mechanic tells you, "There's some transmission noise. You'll have problems with it later on," use that information to seriously bargain down the price. Transmission overhauls are expensive.

If the vehicle has had any serious accidents, you can use that to bargain down the price. But you must specifically ask about a vehicle's repair history. If you don't even ask, they rarely will volunteer such information.

# Mileage

Mileage is another factor. If the vehicle has 80,000 miles on it already, you can be sure that the warranty expired long ago and that the engine has taken a lot of wear. Engine parts will have to be replaced on a fairly constant basis from now on, and will have to be paid out of your own pocket. Remember, used cars are not like wine: They *don't* get better with age. Their problems always get worse.

If you want to be extra sure, you can track the vehicle's repair history by using the VIN (Vehicle Identification Number). Get a copy of the VIN from the dealer or private party, then go to ***www.carfax.com*** on the Internet and get a complete vehicle history report for about $12. This report will give you vehicle specification, vehicle history details, and problem summary.

# Certified by a Mechanic

If you're serious about buying a car, drive it to a garage and get it certified by a mechanic. That examination may cost you $50 or more, but it is an excellent investment if you're not able to spot potential problems yourself. Better to spend $50 and decide—based on the diagnosis—*not* to buy the car, than to buy the car without having it checked and have to shell out $2,000 a couple months later for major repairs.

# Nailing Things Down

When you buy a car from a private owner, it is understood that you are buying it "as is" with no warranties or even guarantees. That's why it's so vital to do a thorough mechanical check up front. Nevertheless, before buying any car, you should write an affidavit saying, "I swear that the car that I am selling, to my knowledge, has no obvious defects, has no rust that I haven't told you about, and the mileage shown on the odometer is correct and accurate." Then ask the owner to sign it, before a notary if possible. Most honest people won't object, and most dishonest ones won't sign it.

# Making the Purchase

When you've settled on the car you want and you and the seller agree on a price, you need to make the deal. It's generally unwise to walk around with thousands of dollars in cash, so offer to make a $100 deposit to hold the deal until you can get a cashier's check from the bank. Unless the seller has had lots of calls on the car, he or she will usually accept your deposit. Be sure to have him or her sign a receipt.

---

                        _____(date)

One hundred dollars ($100) received from

_____ (your name)

as a deposit on the purchase of my car

_____ (make) _____(model)

_____ (year of car) for $_____.\_\_\_ (total sales price).

Balance is due by _____ (tomorrow's date, or

whatever you agree to).

                     _____ (signed)

---

Hold on to this receipt. It's your proof that the car is being held for you and will not be sold to someone else who might come along with a better offer. Now it's time to go to the bank and get a certified or cashier's check to pay for the car. Be sure to list the owner's name on the bank check. If you leave it blank, it's like cash: Lose it and whoever finds it can cash it in.

When you return with the check, be sure the owner writes out a bill of sale, which should list the date, your name, the seller's name, the VIN (Vehicle Identification Number), and the price. The owner should also transfer ownership of the vehicle to you by giving you a Transfer of Ownership form. You'll need the bill of sale and the Transfer of Ownership form to register the car at the Department of Motor Vehicles. Congratulations! You've just bought a car.

# License Fees

License fees normally include vehicle registration fees. If you're buying a car at a dealership, this cost is part and parcel of the price and included in the costs. However, if you're buying from a private individual, you'll need to do this yourself. When the owner sells you the car, he or she must give you the title to the vehicle (via a Transfer of Ownership form) and the vehicle registration papers. You take these down to your local Department of Motor Vehicles, register the car, and pay the transfer fee. You must pay sales tax and license fees in full at this time.

# Smog Certification

Before you can put your vehicle on the road, it has to go through a smog (emissions) check to check for emissions. If you buy a new or used car at a dealership, this should already be taken care of. Also, smog check laws now require that in private-party transactions, the seller must provide you with a smog certificate before or during the time of vehicle transfer. Some sellers will attempt to sell a car without certification. Don't buy.

**CHAPTER 9**

# Make the Purchase— New Cars

"... the contracted agreement, that of the first part..."

"You'll have to discuss that with my lawyers."

# Make the Purchase— New Cars

## Going by the Book

If, after reading all the reasons for buying a used car over a new one, you still decide that you want or need a new car, you should do some careful research to make sure that you don't bite off far more than your bank account can chew.

There are a number of good books which can tell you pretty much everything you need to know about the new vehicle you're considering. They describe the model and make of the car (often accompanied by a photo), and describe its standard features, strengths and weaknesses, performance, passenger accommodation, and value for your money. You can borrow books such as the *Consumer Report's* annual auto issue, the *Kelley Blue Book*, etc. from a library and study them at your leisure.

## Searching Cyber Space

You can also do research on the Internet. There are a number of sites on the World Wide Web that tell you whatever you need to know about new car ratings. A good place to start is the CyberWheels website at **www.cyberwheels.com** Cyberwheels links to a wide range of automotive sites by category. It can take you to **www.edmunds.com** to check out prices, to individual manufacturer's home pages to check out their glossy (often high-tech) photos of cars, and even go to **www.carwizard.com** to figure out your financing. Also check **www.autosite.com** for the *Ultimate Automotive Buyer's Guide*.

Print out all the information you need. You're now much better able to make an informed purchase.

# Frills and Features

If you want extra frills that your potential purchase doesn't have, you can often have those features added at the factory before the car is shipped to you. You can choose the color and upholstery, have a super stereo system put in, add air-conditioning, seat warmers, automatic windows, and sometimes even have a sunroof put in. Of course, adding these features is going to *cost!* Be sure to find out exactly what each feature will add to the overall price.

If you've already chosen the car off the lot and want some frills added, it's usually best to buy these parts separately and either add them yourself or get an honest mechanic to do so. Dealerships often talk new buyers into paying $1,000 to have some frill installed, when the part itself cost only $600.

# Warranties

One of the reasons people buy new instead of used—despite the huge, sudden drop in value the first year—is the comprehensive warranty that comes with the new car. If you've faithfully had checkups on your car and something that wasn't supposed to go wrong with it early in the game *does* go wrong, manufacturers will pay to have it repaired. So if your engine mounts give out and your motor crashes on the road, they promise to repair that.

You need to take a look at what manufacturers include under their basic warranty, and be aware of when that warranty will run out. Remember, one of the reasons you're buying new instead of used is *because* of the extra protection of that warranty. So it pays to know exactly what you're getting for the extra thousands you're paying.

When you buy a new car, you should be covered under the factory warranty for regular checkups, safety inspections, and oil changes for a specified length of time. The schedule will be listed in your owner's manual, but it is up to you to remember to go back to your dealership's service department and take advantage of these checkups.

A dealership warranty is different from the manufacturer's warranty, and usually refers to an extended warranty you can get after the original manufacturer's warranty has run out.

# Deductibles

A *deductible* is the amount of money your service contract makes you pay to fix something covered under the warranty. You may feel you shouldn't have to pay anything at all, since the engine wasn't even supposed to have that fault, but paying a $50 deductible is still a lot better than paying the $2,500 for the full repair.

# Factory Recalls

Sometimes after a car has been on the market for a while, the manufacturers begin repeatedly receiving the same complaint from customers. For example, they find out that driving a 1997 Lemonella over gravel roads in excess of 40 mph causes the backseat to unhinge and the trunk door to fly open, throwing any groceries or spare tires into the dust. So a factory recall goes out, and all proud owners of '97 Lemonellas get a notice in the mail telling them to take their car back to their dealers for a free repair.

# Signing the Papers

If you negotiated an acceptable price for the car you wanted, now is the time to sign the papers. Remember, however, this is a legal, binding contract. Once your signature is on the dotted line, you are obligated to fulfill it. So before you sign, take the time to read it over and make sure that everything is in order and that no new charges or surprise fees are trying to sneak themselves onto the page. If you have questions, ask the dealer. Make sure the contract you sign says what you want it to say.

# CHAPTER 10

# Tips for Long-Lasting Vehicles

"I think you got oil everywhere else except in the engine!"

# Tips for Long-Lasting Vehicles

## Regular Checkups

Regular maintenance and service checks are extremely important. For a while, it may seem that a service check, costing you $50–$75 dollars every three months, is an unnecessary expense. After all, the mechanic may not be finding anything wrong. So what's the point? Or if he *does* find something—bummer—it's just one more bill to pay.

Invariably, however, you'll be thankful for those checkups. Like the day the mechanic informs you, "Good thing you brought it in! We discovered a major oil leak. We can fix it now for $200, but in two weeks it would've cost you $3,000." Or the day they discover your weasely little engine mounts working themselves loose.

Besides—and this is a big besides—if the car is still covered by a warranty but you haven't done these checkups as stipulated, the manufacturer has the right to void your warranty and refuse to pay for your claims. Now *that* can be costly!

Even if it's not time for a regular tune-up, if your engine starts making any rattling, clanging, hissing, whumping, or squealing sounds; has trouble starting; or begins leaking oil, get it into a garage. It costs to make repairs, but it costs even more not to make them in time.

## Changing Oil

It's recommended that you change your engine oil every three months or every 3,000 miles, whichever comes first. Read your car's manual for more information. This isn't an area where you want to skimp to save money or time. If you don't know how to do it yourself, have a friend do it. Or combine your regular oil change with your regular tune-up.

# Tires: Tread and Air

Keep an eye on your tires. Never allow them to get so bald that the tread is almost gone. This is just begging for a blowout or even a serious accident. Also, watch your air pressure. Know how many PSI (pounds per square inch) of air you should keep in your tires during summer, and how much during winter. If you don't know, ask. Keeping your tires properly inflated can improve your vehicle's fuel economy.

# Water in the Radiator

Check the water level in your radiator regularly. Make sure to check it when your engine is cold, not after it's been running and is hot, otherwise you could get scalded. If the water level gets down too low, it can cause serious problems and require hefty repairs. And if your vehicle requires a special type of antifreeze for winter or summer, make sure that's what it gets. A thirsty car is a grumpy car.

# Batteries

The same is true with batteries. If your battery has a leak and all the water drains out, your car won't start and the battery will be ruined and need to be replaced. This is no fun, but it is especially bad if you're out in the middle of nowhere or if you have a car full of friends headed for fun at the beach.

# Lights

If your headlights, taillights, signal lights, or running lights are out or on the blink, take care of them right away. This is a safety issue. Headlights that aren't working could get you pulled over by the police. Signal lights that aren't working could get you *run* over by a semi!

If the warning lights on your dashboard light up, they're not just lighting up to add variety or to look pretty. They're trying to warn you that something is wrong with your car, and that you need to take it in to a garage.

# Winterizing Your Car

If you live in Key Largo, winterizing your car is not something you even think of. Winter? What's *that?* But if you live in Idaho or Maine or North Saskatchewan—and especially if you live in Alaska—winterizing your car is serious business. But even if you live in areas where the temperature doesn't often drop below freezing, this isn't something you can safely ignore.

When winter is coming, be very sure that you put antifreeze in your radiator or the water could freeze and crack the radiator. You also need to make sure your tires have adequate treads. If they're nearly bald and the roads have snow or ice, watch out! And if you don't keep chains in your trunk (they may not be allowed in your state) or even a snow shovel, at least carry some cardboard to stick under the wheels when your car gets stuck.

# In Case of an Accident

If you have a major accident and it was your fault, your insurance will pay for it, true, but they will then jack up your monthly rates to compensate for what you made them pay. That's why, if you're only involved in a small accident, it's sometimes worth paying for the other person's repairs out of your pocket, rather than see your insurance rate shoot up.

But of course, the best way to avoid all such expenses is to drive defensively: Don't squeal out into the thick of a traffic stampede; do signal before you change lanes; don't speed on a rain-slick highway; don't try to pass on a blind corner; pay attention when the light turns red. You know, all that commonsense stuff.

# When You're the Victim

Let's say you're a careful driver and you never take chances. But one day you're driving through a green light and some driver, intent on making a right turn, roars out into your lane and broadsides you. What do you do? The first thing to do is check that no one is injured, including the other driver. And watch out for traffic!

It's often a good idea not to move the vehicles after an accident. When the police come, you'll want them to see the exact positions, point of impact, etc.—since this helps establish responsibility. However, if the accident happened in the middle of the street and was a mere fender bender, it's usually best to move your cars out of the way.

If the other driver drives off, write down the license number. This is called a *hit-and-run*. If other motorists saw what happened and stopped, ask them if they would be witnesses. If so, take their names and telephone numbers. Then report the accident to the police.

However, if the other driver stops as he should, inspect the damage to your vehicle and his, then make a nonaggressive suggestion that you should probably exchange information. Write down his name, phone number and address, the license number of his car, and the number of his driver's license.

Another reason it pays to get the name and phone number of a witness is in case the driver that hit you is in denial and argues that it was *your* fault. When the police arrive, tell your side of the story calmly and clearly and get others to corroborate.

# Leave My Insurance Out of This

The other driver may agree that he was at fault, but if he lets the insurance company pay for your repairs, they in turn would make him pay huge premiums. Plus the accident would appear on his driving record. To avoid this, he may ask if he can pay for the repair out of his own pocket. This may be a reasonable request. However—

Don't immediately agree on an amount. Tell him you'll take your car to a garage for a repair estimate. Then when you phone him, if he agrees to the amount, ask for either cash or a certified check.

Secondly, tell him that you and your passengers will

need to go to a doctor for a checkup to make sure no one was injured. Letting the other person off the hook may seem like the "forgiving" thing to do, but a few weeks later your slightly strained neck might develop into long-term neck pain, headaches, and vision problems. If you settled on the spot for repair costs, you now can't claim the extended medical coverage you need—and which his insurance policy was there to provide—nor will you be reimbursed for the workdays you end up missing.

State laws may vary, but in many cases, if an accident causes more than $2,000 damage, you are required by law to report it to the police within forty-eight hours.

## If You Were at Fault

OK, let's reverse the scenario. A lady was driving through the green light. *You* roared out on a red light and broadsided her. Now what do you do? Besides repent, I mean. Again, check that no one was injured, especially the other driver.

If you were in the wrong, own up and apologize sincerely. You don't, however, have to accept abuse. Neither do you have to remain silent if she is wildly waving her arms at you, then, the instant the police arrive, leans against her car and moans, "Whiplash . . ." You would be amazed at people who pretend to be seriously injured, treat a minor accident like a winning lotto ticket, sue for millions, and retire early. So stand up for the truth.

## Ownership and Contentment

For a Christian, "owning" a car is really an oxymoron. As believers, we and every material thing in our possession belong to God. We're just stewards over the things, and God has merely entrusted them to our care. We may argue that we were the ones who worked hard and earned the money to buy the car, but even the ability to earn money is a gift from God (Deuteronomy 8:17–18).

Since we're just stewards over God's money, we ought

to consult Him in prayer over every vehicle we're considering spending His money on. God often allows us a lot of choice in the matter and Psalm 37:4 says, "He will give you the desires of your heart," but the condition to this, of course, is that you "delight yourself in the Lord," meaning putting Him first.

We should also trust God to provide the vehicle we need. This doesn't mean we can shirk our responsibility of looking for the best car, doing diligent research, and carefully checking things out, but it *does* mean that if we're praying for a fish, God is not about to give us a snake (Matthew 7:9–10). Likewise, if we're praying for a good car, God is not the One who just sent that junker our way. So don't buy it. He may not send you a shiny new sports car, but God will send you a car that meets your needs.

# Glossary

**Deductible:** The fee you pay to have repairs made if your vehicle is covered by a warranty (e.g., you pay only $50 of a $1,500 repair).

**Depreciation:** The amount of value or worth a vehicle loses over time.

**Down payment:** Money you pay up front (usually 10 percent of the total price), when you finance the purchase of a car.

**Financing:** Financing means getting a bank to loan you the money to buy a car.

**Leasing:** Renting a vehicle for a specified period of time, usually two to three years.

**Make:** The name of the car manufacturer: Ford, Chevrolet, Toyota, etc.

**Model:** The specific *kind* of car: an Impala, a Continental, etc.

**New used car:** A previously owned car that is still in very good shape.

**Sticker price:** The price written on the car that the dealer hopes you'll pay.

**Tune-ups:** This is when you regularly take your vehicle in to a service station to have your engine checked, oil changed, etc.

**VIN (Vehicle Identification Number):** Every vehicle has its own individual number written on its papers, on the dashboard, and under the hood.

**Warranty, manufacturer's:** A guarantee that if anything goes wrong with one of their new cars within a specified time, the manufacturer will fix it.

**Warranty, extended:** A service contract made to get extra coverage after the manufacturer's warranty has expired.

# Index

**Larry Burkett's Stewardship for the Family**™ provides the practical tips and tools that children and parents need to understand biblical principles of stewardship. Its goal is *"Teaching Kids to Manage God's Gifts—Time, Talents and Treasures."* Stewardship for the Family™ materials are adapted from the works of best-selling author on business and personal finances, **Larry Burkett**. Larry is the author of more than 60 books and hosts the radio programs "Money Matters" and "How to Manage Your Money," aired on more than 1,100 outlets worldwide. Visit Larry's website at www.mm4kids.org